Other Books By The Author

Winner for Best Inspirational in
Pacific Book Award 2020

JUST A THOUGHT

RICHARD BYRD

VOLUME 1

Just A Thought
Volume 1

Copyright © 2022 by Richard Byrd.

Paperback ISBN: 978-1-63812-390-3
Ebook ISBN: 978-1-63812-391-0

All rights reserved. No part in this book may be produced and transmitted in any form or by any means, electronic, or mechanical, including photocopying, recording, or by any information storage and retrieval system, without permission in writing from the copyright owner.

The views expressed in this work are solely those of the author and do not necessarily reflect the views of the publisher hereby disclaims any responsibility for them.

Published by Pen Culture Solutions 08/13/2022

Pen Culture Solutions
1-888-727-7204 (USA)
1-800-950-458 (Australia)
support@penculturesolutions.com

Just a thought 1

*Existence is only
a reflection
of the flesh...
Just a thought*

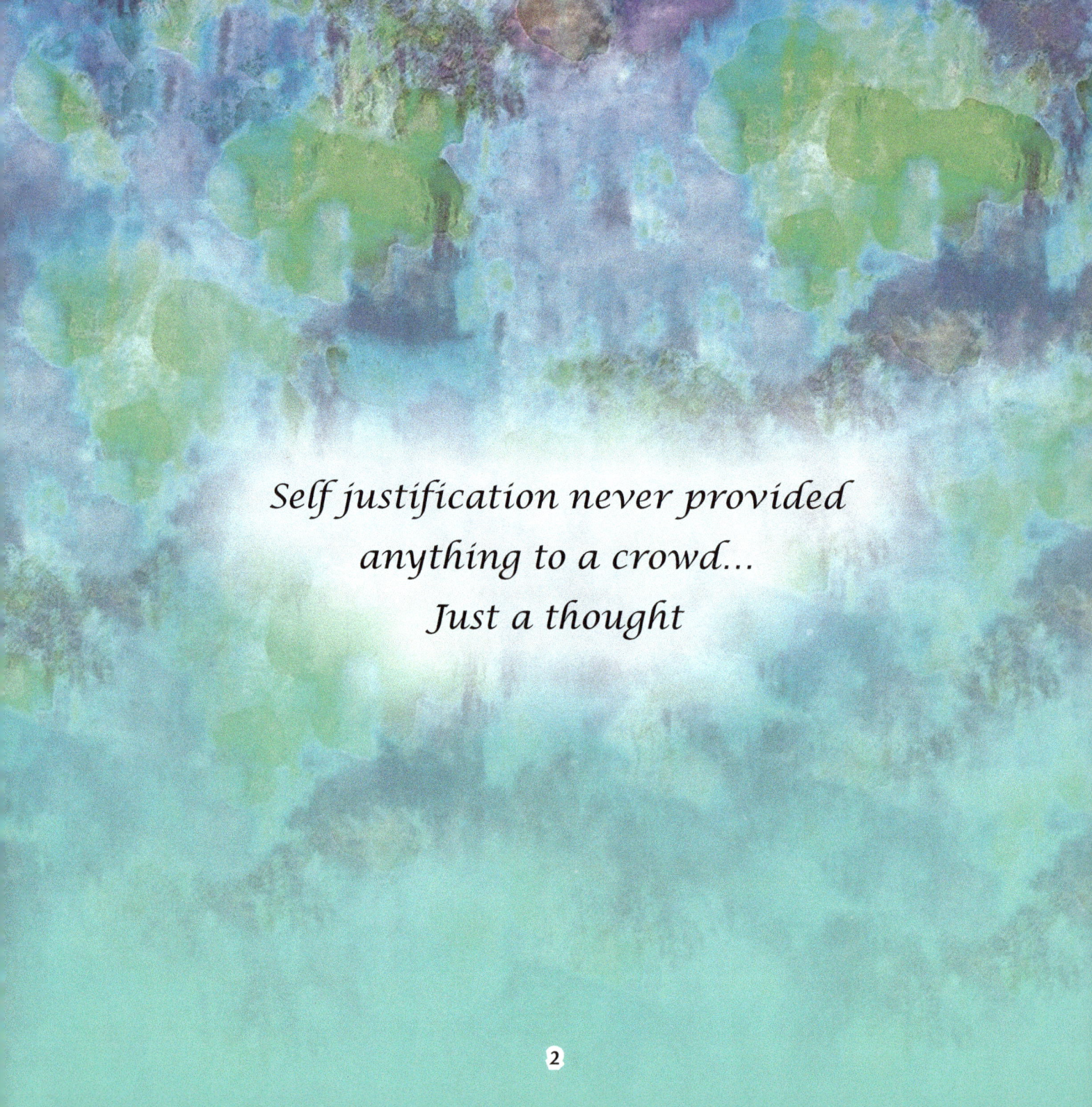

Self justification never provided
anything to a crowd...
Just a thought

*Inventory of ourselves
is always necessary
when we are being judgmental
of someone else...
Just a thought*

*Hope is a tremendous obstacle
to someone who looks
forward to failure...
Just a thought*

*Hope is a tremendous goal
to reach for a hopeless mind,
our biggest defects
are centered in the way we think…
Just a thought*

*Things are taken
without your permission
when you take them for granted...
Just a thought*

*Moving beyond your counterparts
or friends, to outgrow
the usual environments,
is to mature...
Just a thought*

You will be noticed
if you stop trying
so hard to be seen...
Just a thought

Resentment is a spiritual disease,
it allows you to take
on someone else's issues
without your permission...
Just a thought

*Excuses are tools of denial,
used to build monuments of failure and
those who specializes in them seldom
amount to any kind of status
or responsibility...
Just a thought*

*Imagination is what dreams are made of,
it's a basis to explore an unknown universe
to help enhance our spiritual awareness to
find some knowledge that normally
would be out of reach...
Just a thought*

When the story becomes a lie
then who's telling it...
Just a thought

*Rebirth and renewal of the mind will always open new horizons to explore...
Just a thought*

*The personal life, that last life
didn't have social situations that were
worth while to continue and nobody
could depend on us, so dramatically
we changed our way of thinking
to improve the atmosphere, by giving
back what was freely given to us
and then we could live life
on life's terms once more...
Just a thought*

Money and friends are a lot alike,
easy to get but hard to keep...
Just a thought

In any relationship we must know that
love, comfort and support
will last longer than
any materialistic idea...
Just a thought

*Some people think
that a sexual relationship
is part of growing up
but to their surprise
they realize to late
that immorality isn't a way
to find immortality...
Just a thought*

Comments are just opinions
without much thought behind them...
Just a thought

Your past didn't open the gates of heaven
to let you in,
it opened the gates of hades
to let you out...
Just a thought

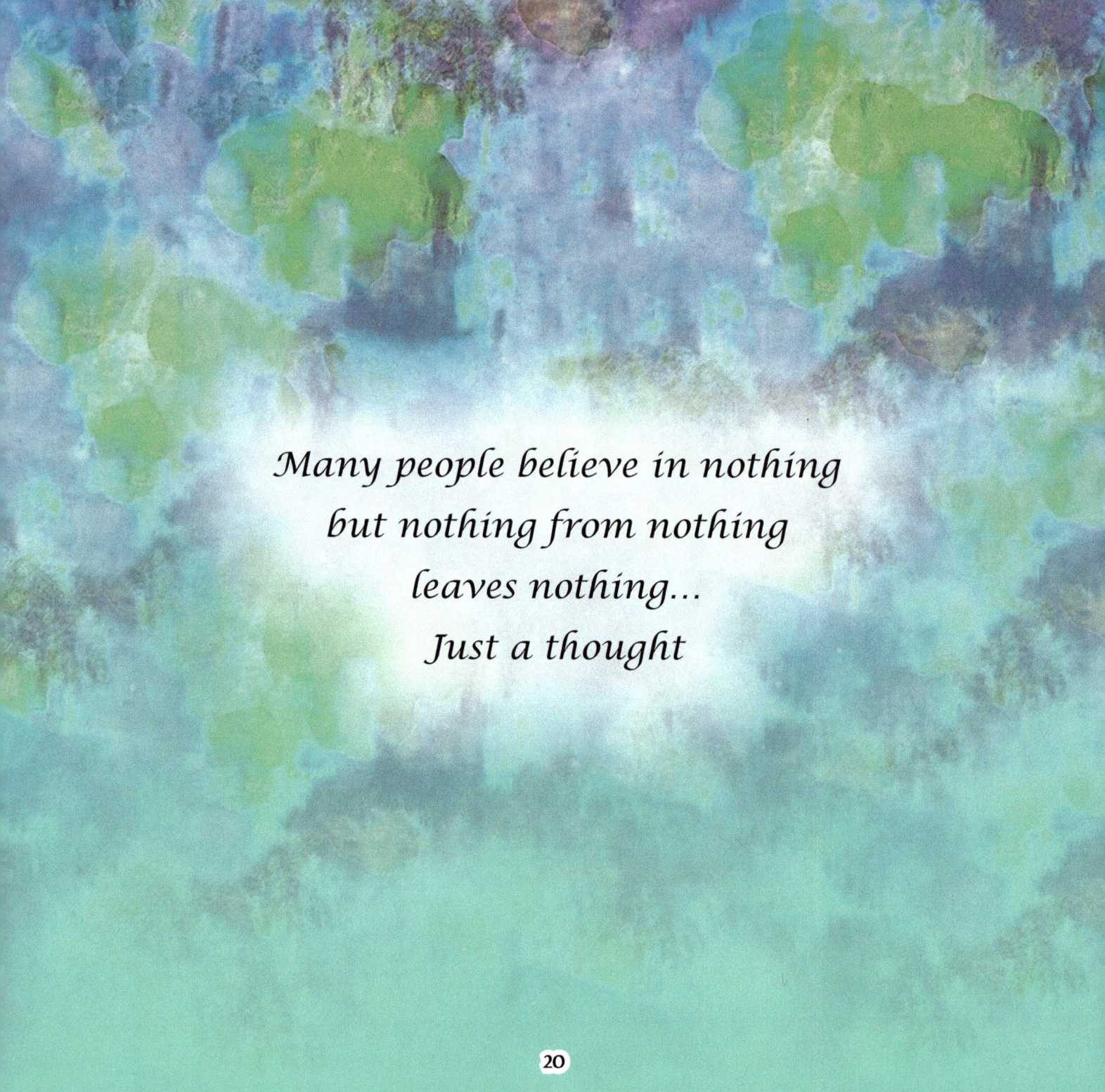

Many people believe in nothing
but nothing from nothing
leaves nothing...
Just a thought

*Even though you are a religious person
it doesn't mean that
you are spiritually connected...
Just a thought*

*Temptation is the worm
that the apple keeps hidden…
Just a thought*

Sometimes people get what they want
instead of what they need
and at the end of the day
they lose whatever they had...
Just a thought

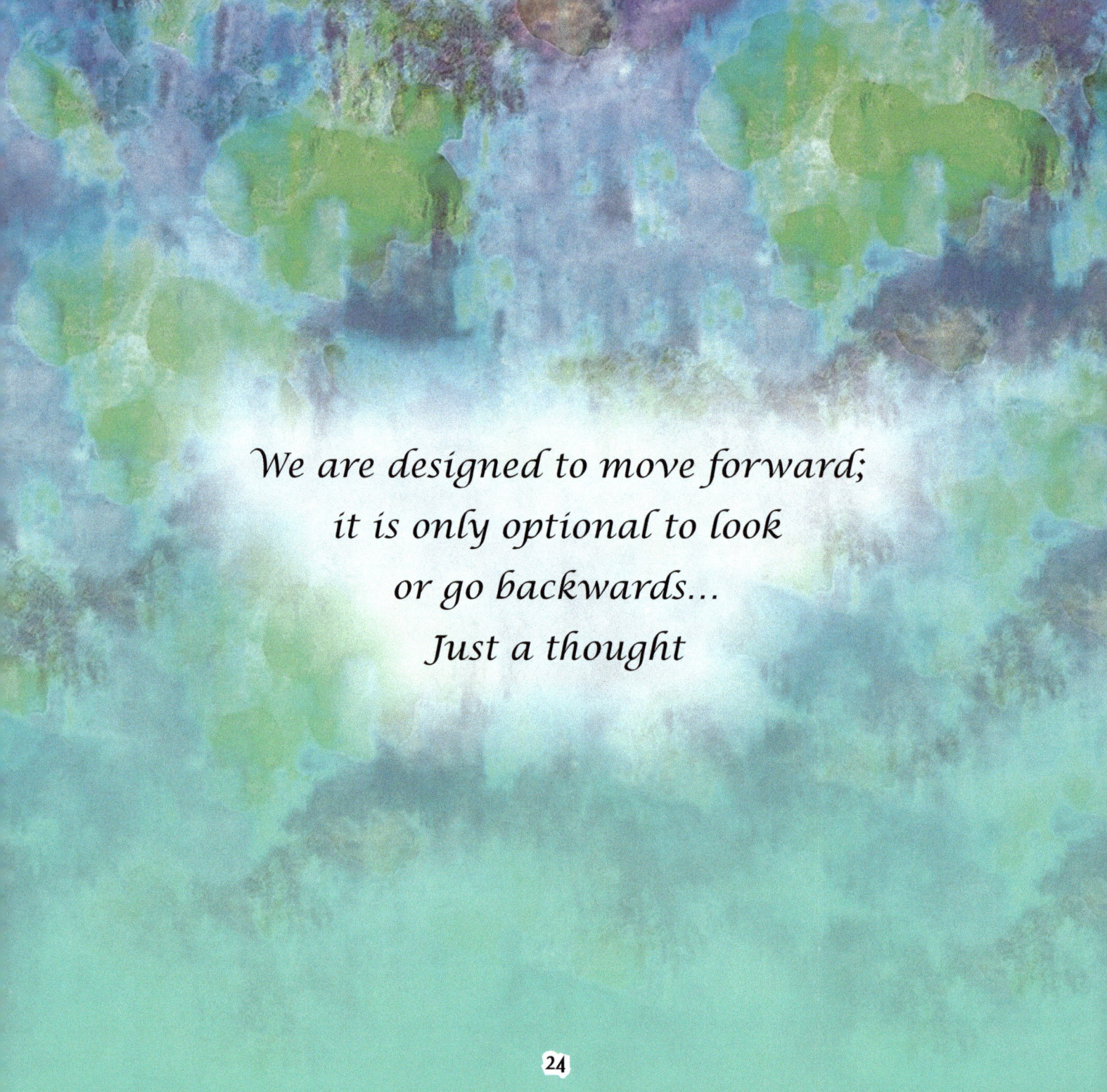

We are designed to move forward;
it is only optional to look
or go backwards...
Just a thought

*It takes a system of checks and balances
to understand how aware we are
to be secure enough
in whatever life has to offer...*
J.A.TH

*Good judgment
becomes common sense
when you have an open mind…
Just a thought*

Pain can only hold you hostage
if you won't let it go...
Just a thought

*It's better to be poor with integrity
than to be rich with no friends...
Just a thought*

*I've took my eyes off yesterday
and threw the keys away,
tomorrow has no fear for me
since I have today...
Just a thought*

The delusion is when your mind tells you
that the allusion is real,
as if to say that your girlfriend or boyfriend
is your husband or wife...
Just a thought

A child learns discipline from the adults
but if the adults doesn't plant the seeds,
they receive no harvest...
Just a thought

*Some will panic in desperate times,
but desperation is only a false state of
mind, that has lost its faith
for that moment when to be strong
wasn't entirely enough...
Just a thought*

*Death is never final
for those who are
just passing on...
Just a thought*

*Fantastic stories
can come from bad decisions
and wrong turns...
Just a thought*

The awesomeness' of one individual
can be immeasurable
depending on who's
taking the measurements...
Just a thought

*Self justifications
never helped the accused...
Just a thought*

*If I could turn back
the hands of time,
I would lose the reality
of my own experiences...
Just a thought*

*We can never pay
for our own peace of mind
at the expense of someone else...
Just a thought*

We know what we know
but when we take suggestions,
we learn more...
Just a thought

A fool is always right in his or her own mind... Just a thought

To be warm hearted, generous
and friendly towards others
is to be kind with whoever
comes our way...
Just a thought

Nothing changes who you use to be
accept who you are becoming today...
Just a thought

Isolation is a demonstration of a situation that someone would love to get out of...
Just a thought

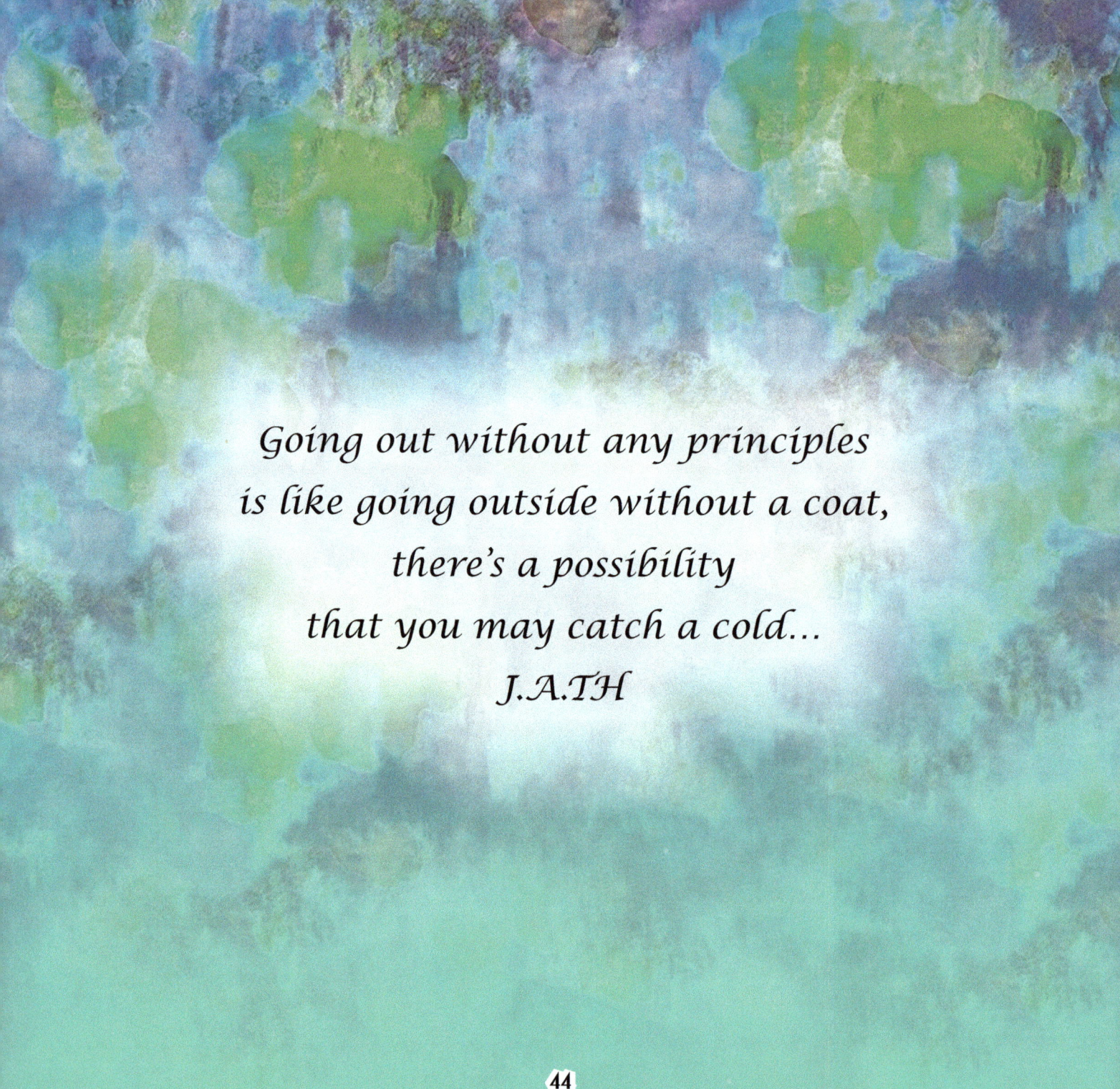

Going out without any principles
is like going outside without a coat,
there's a possibility
that you may catch a cold...
J.A.TH

*Somewhere between
nowhere and goodbye
is moving on...
Just a thought*

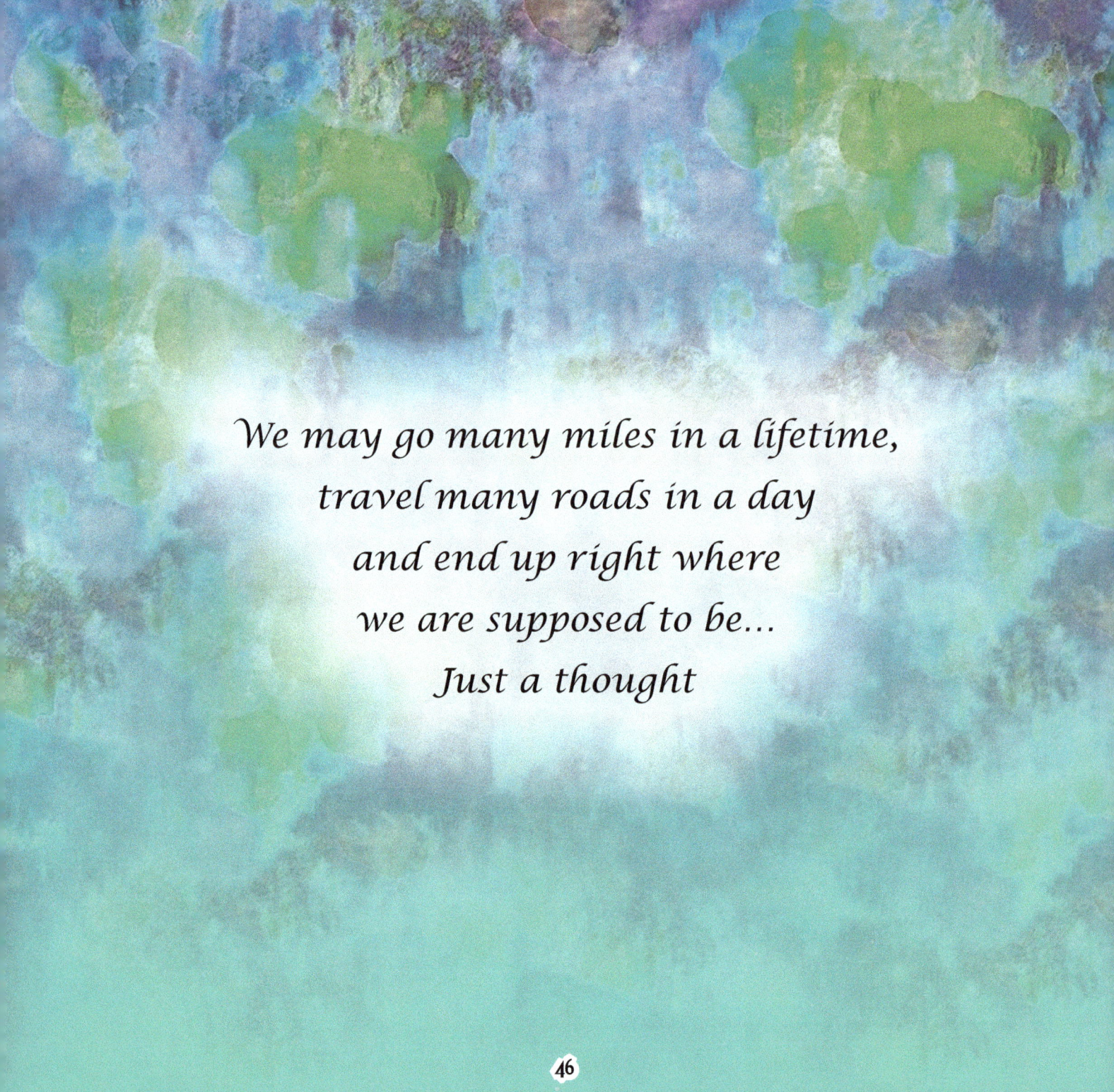

We may go many miles in a lifetime,
travel many roads in a day
and end up right where
we are supposed to be...
Just a thought

Knowledge is what we know, information is what we seek to know, and experience is the active participation of them both... Just a thought

Jealousy is a state of mind
in which trust is not included
and insecurities take control...
just a thought

GOD may take you places
that old friends may not be able to follow
when you find your purpose...
just a thought

Never push people away
just because you are going
through something,
all that does is leave you alone...
Just a thought

*Reconciliation is the peace
that comes with forgiveness...
Just a thought*

DEPENDENCY – The phenomenon
is like an imaginary image
that sometimes consist of a dependency, of
emotional imbalances that stimulates
the brain into a consumption,
of a false release, of a sensational
satisfaction and it is never enough...
Just a thought

*Being single is a choice
that very few people
likes' to keep…
Just a thought*

*A problem is just an issue
that haven't been faced
with a solution...
Just a thought*

The image in the mirror
is only a reflection
of the truth...
just a thought

The clay pot can be broken now
and then just to be mended back
together again...
just a thought

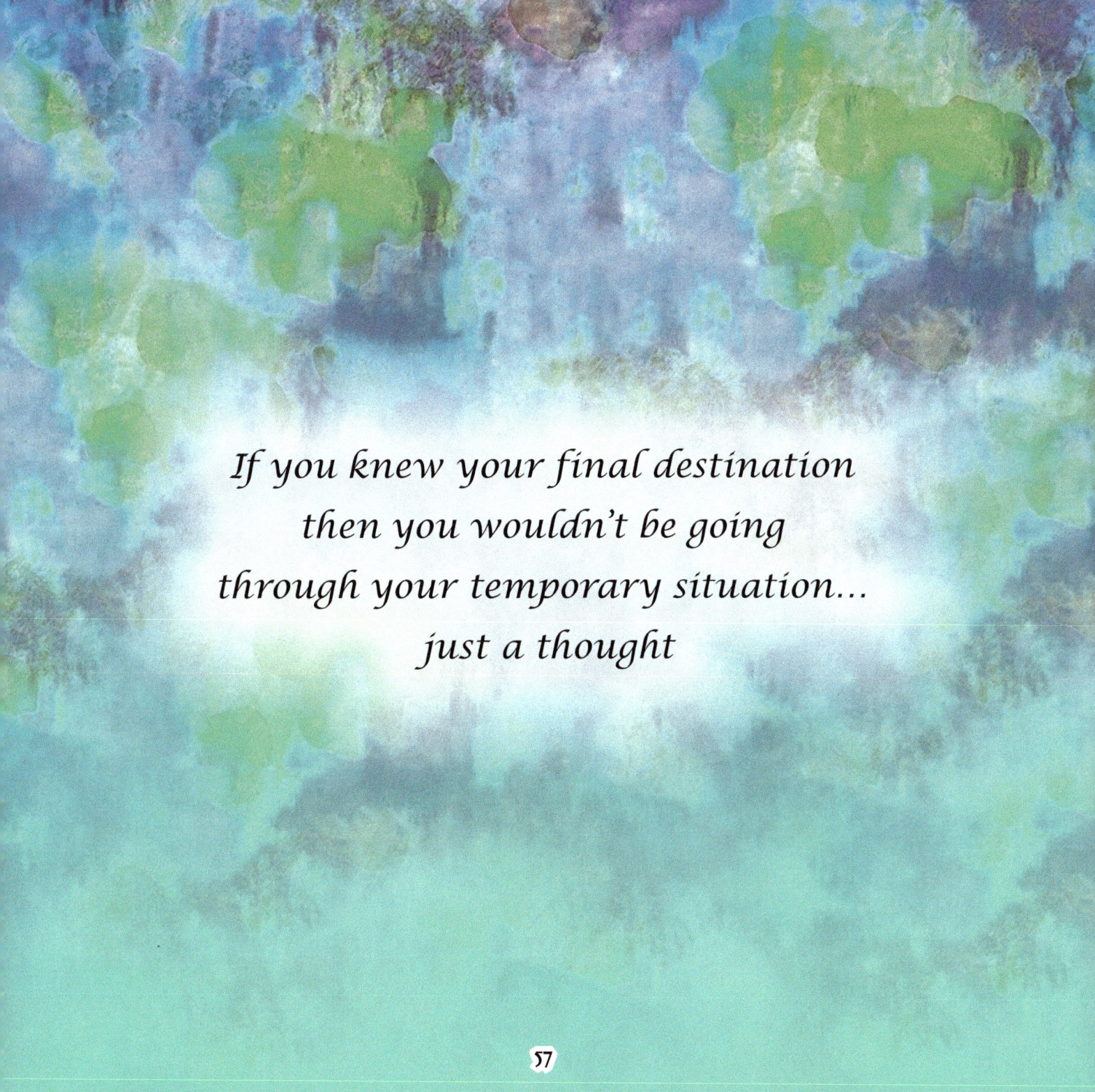

*If you knew your final destination
then you wouldn't be going
through your temporary situation...
just a thought*

The best way to overcome
everyone else's problems
is to not make them your own...
just a thought

*Seeking material possessions
is like looking for life
in all the wrong places
you can't take it with you...
just a thought*

When the time comes
it will never be about
how you died or from what
But how did you live...
just a thought

*Just like a mountain
cannot be moved by the storm
you should not be moved
by what they say or think...
just a thought*

A curious mind cannot be stopped
when it wants to know
Why is this or that...
Just a thought

Friends are never lost when associated with good memories... just a thought

*Nobody is born knowing that
hardships and mistakes
would be the pathway
to peace and stability...
just a thought*

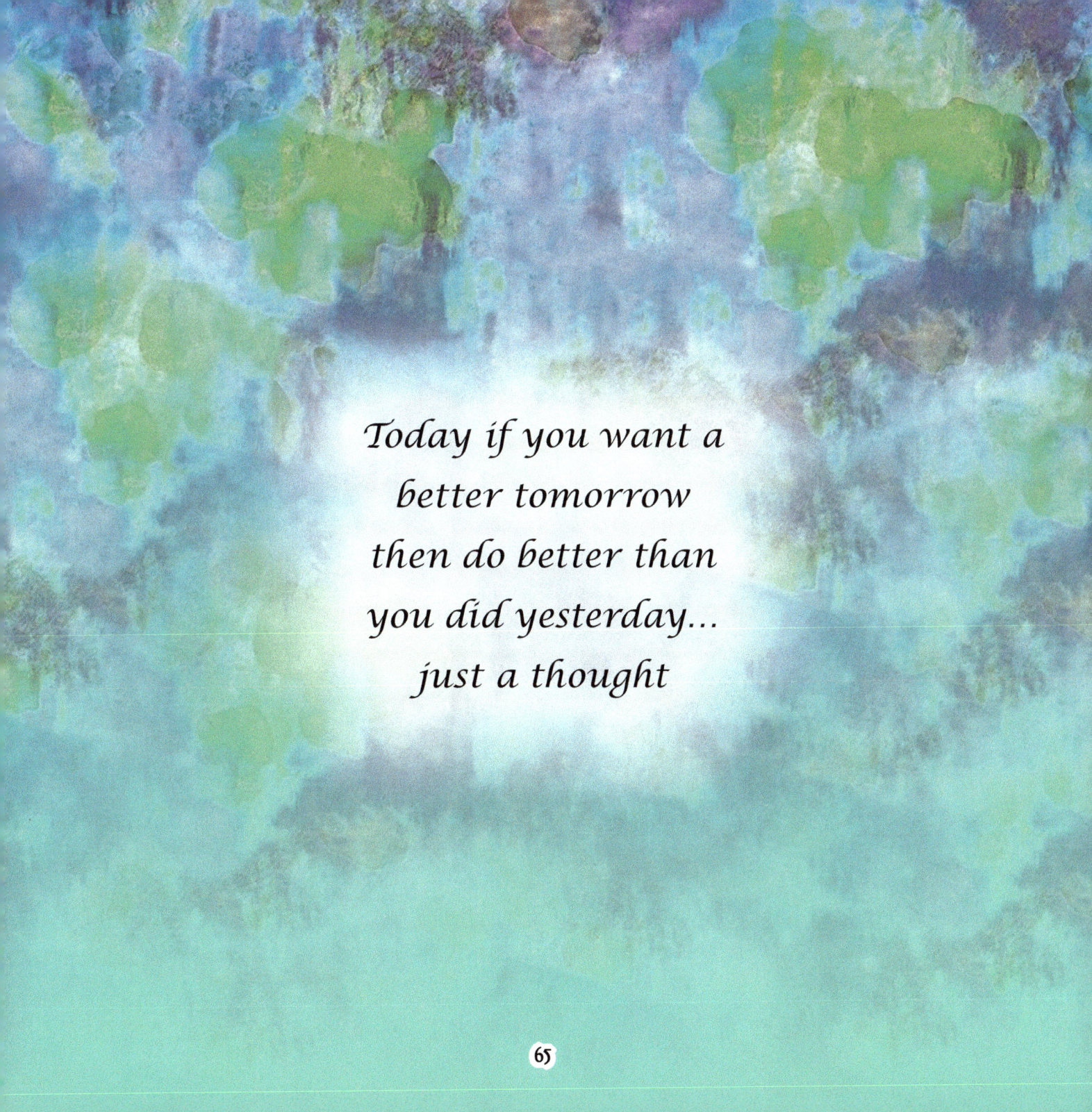

Today if you want a better tomorrow then do better than you did yesterday... just a thought

*Living the dream
on Plan B…
just a thought*

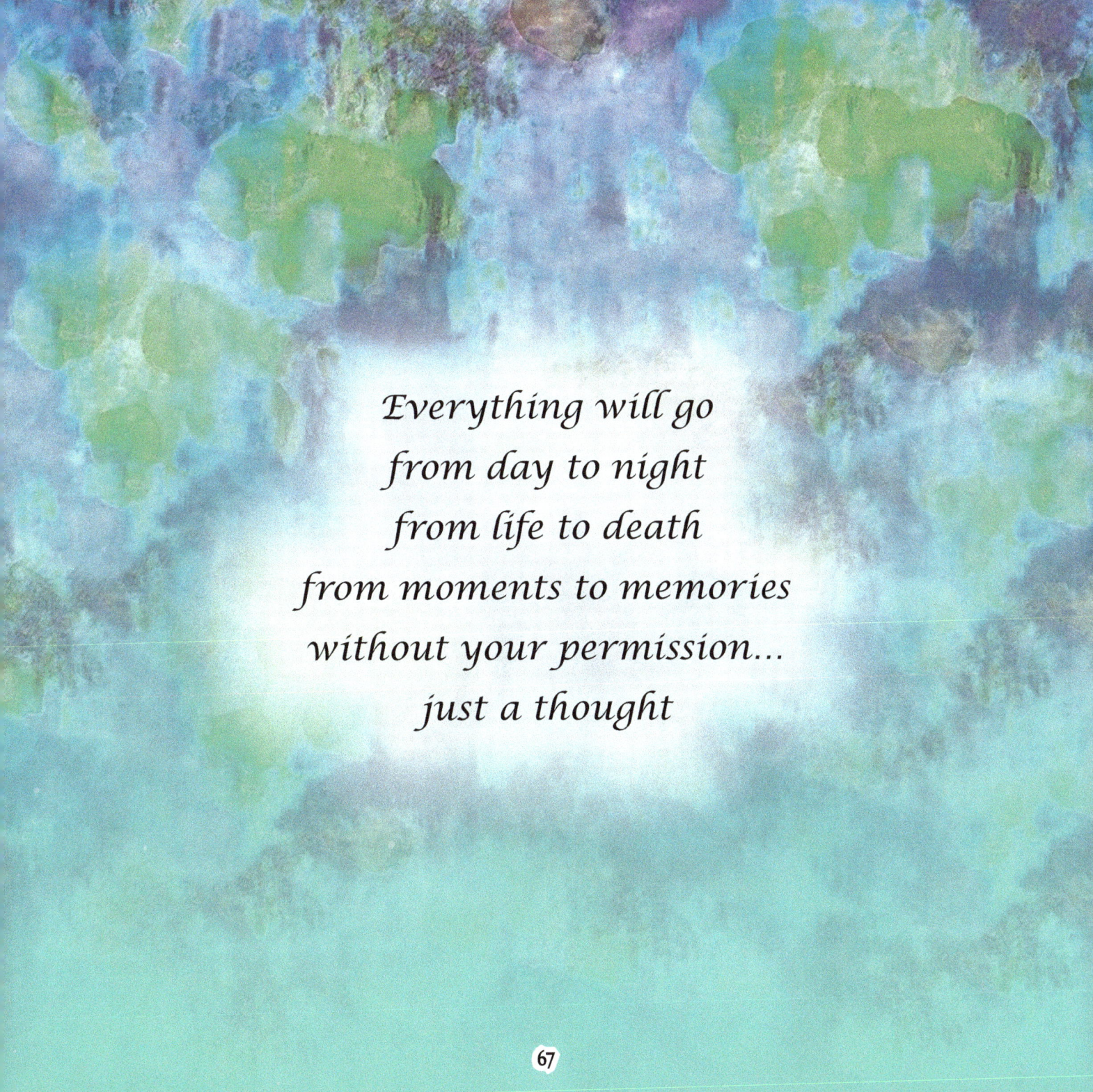

*Everything will go
from day to night
from life to death
from moments to memories
without your permission...
just a thought*

The best thing about being human
is that there is a greater version
of yourself just waiting to be released...
just a thought

*Physical feelings
will forget about the touch
once it has been released...
just a thought*

Sometimes God will move
a person out of your life
to clear the way for
someone better...
just a thought

*Understanding and knowledge
are very different
you can have knowledge of me
and no understanding of who I am...
Just a thought*

There's a beginning and an end
everything else disappears
in between...
Just a thought

They get rich off other people's sufferings and called it charity... just a thought

*Like the spokes on a wheel
we all have an equal part
to play and a purpose...
Just a thought*

A bad day is just another day to do a little more readjusting... Just a thought

*People pleasers will never say what's on their mind...
Just a thought*

If you think that you are a loser
then you've already lost
your only limits are the obstacles
in your mind or thinking...
Just a thought

*Our primary focus
should never become
our secondary goals...
just a thought*

All dignity is lost
when the fool
shows up...
Just a thought

*The greatest value
that no currency
could ever have is trust...
Just a thought*

*The biggest hearts
are within the children;
humbleness is to love
as a child loves...
Just a thought*

Single is not a choice or a decision it's a cry for companionship... Just a thought

*Luck is only the illusion
of the chance that it may
or may not happen...
just a thought*

Where you were
and where you are
will never end up
in the same place…
Just a thought

Rejection will push you away just like broken promises... just a thought

A wise person once said that
if you don't have any experience
on the matter then just listen
you may just learn something...
just a thought

Mistakes will be made, imperfection is the root of being human... just a thought

*Discipline isn't just an opportunity
to symbolize with our
self-improvement in life,
it's accompanied by counter questioning
and continuing with our
own self-examination...
just a thought*

Dead weight needs
to be left behind
even though it may
feel like you may
have just lost your
best friend...
just a thought

Specially and specifically designed,
fundamentally sound,
human with every I dotted,
and every T crossed we are made,
no instrument or tool has ever been created
with such detail or functionality...
just a thought

We must remove the impurities
within the elements of our spirits
to process the changes
that we would want to take place
within our souls...
just a thought

Dead Space and a lifetime of experience is a lesson learned... just a thought

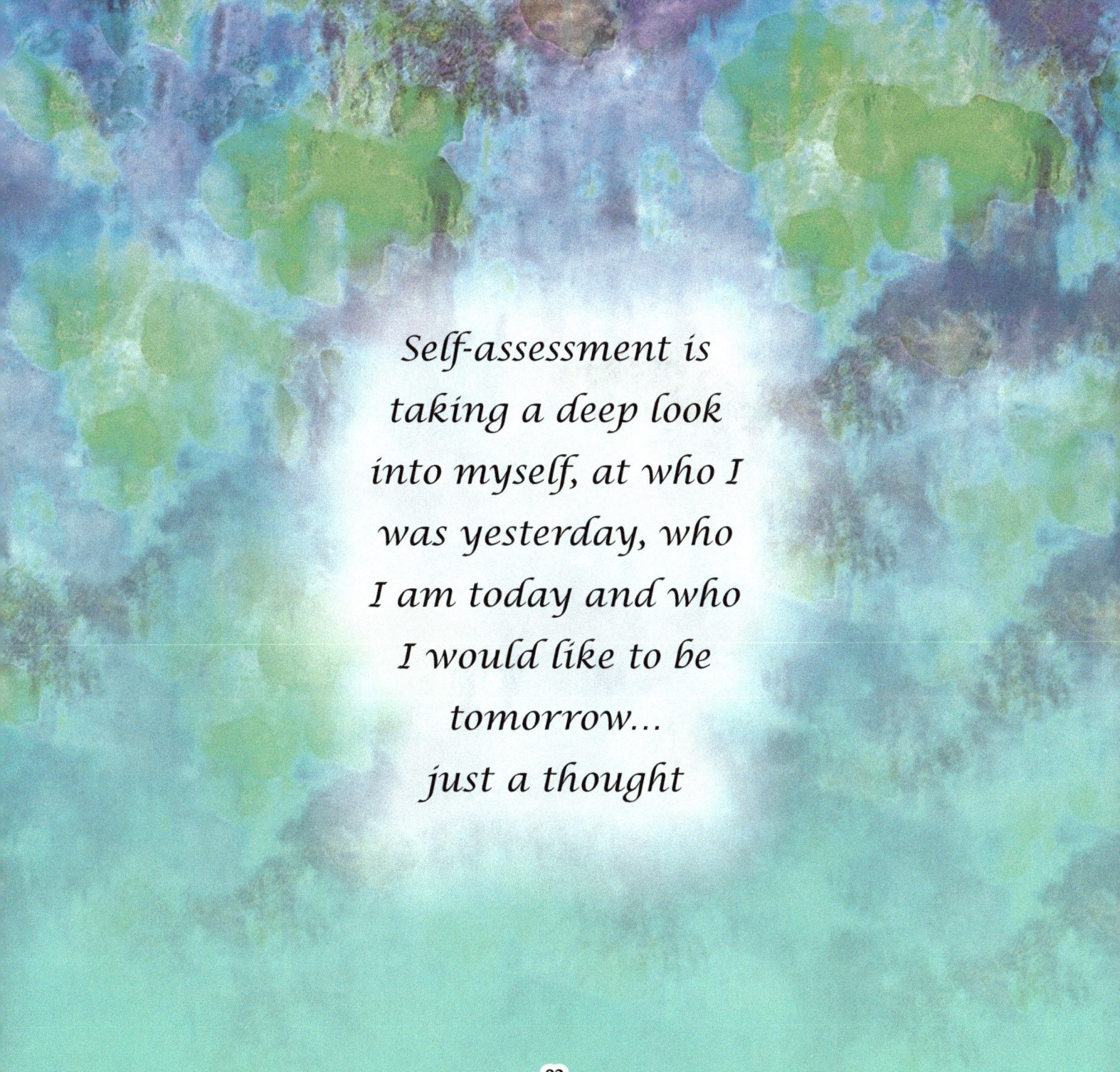

Self-assessment is taking a deep look into myself, at who I was yesterday, who I am today and who I would like to be tomorrow...
just a thought

See without hindrance, to get rid of the mist and haze that is obstructing your vision, look and envision with love and truth... just a thought

*Be like a sponge
and soak in the joy
of living...
just a thought*

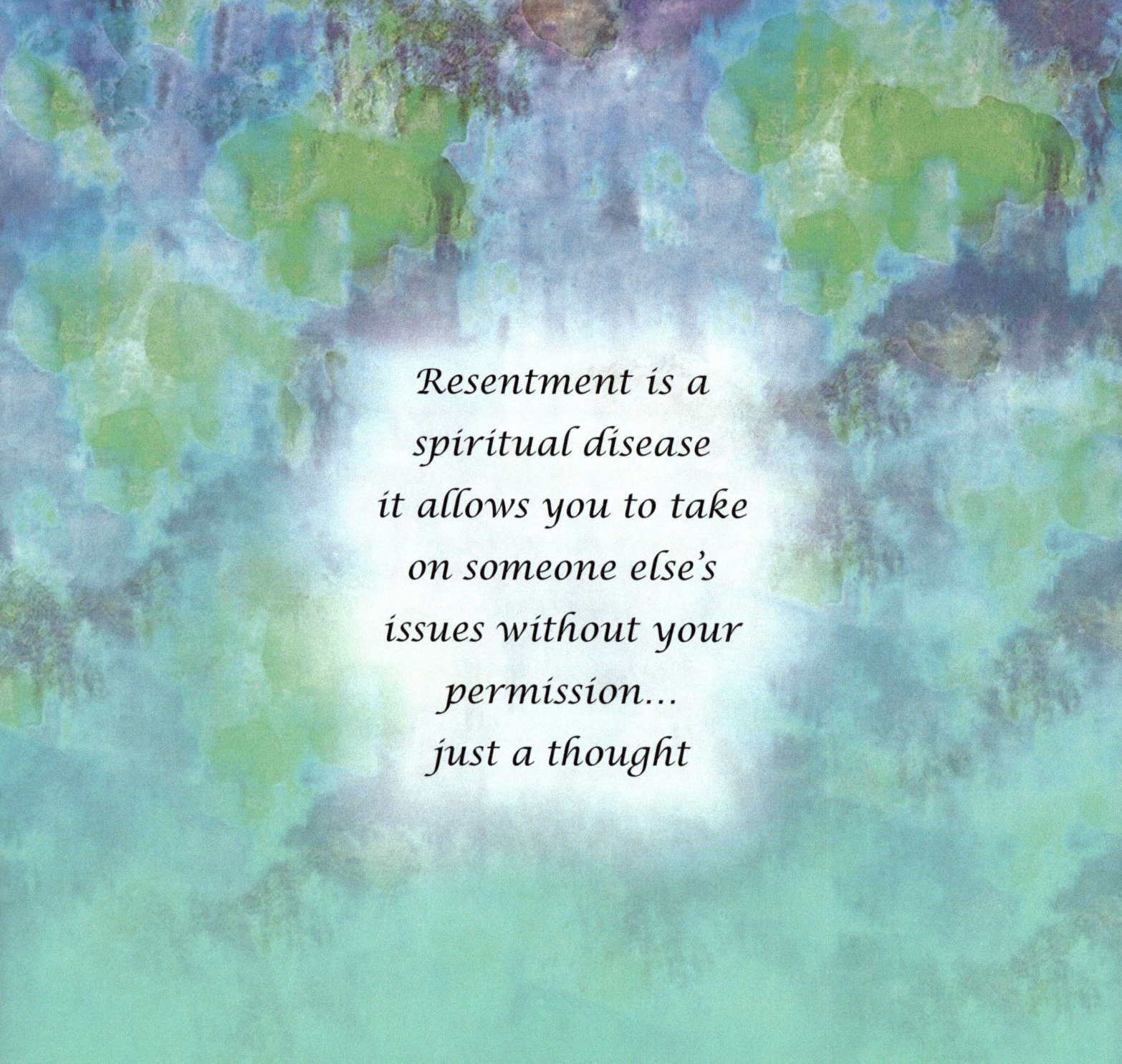

Resentment is a
spiritual disease
it allows you to take
on someone else's
issues without your
permission...
just a thought

People say
let's just get along,
but nobody is willing
to take the first step...
just a thought

You can sit back
and watch things happen
or you can get up
and help make them happen...
just a thought

Because they say I love you
it doesn't mean that they are
in love with you,
love and lust
are not the same...
just a thought

ABOUT THE AUTHOR

Richard Byrd debuts in the literary limelight with the release of "Just A Thought" (published by AuthorHouse in July 2018). Inspired from his personal experiences, the self-help book that is set for a new marketing push, aims to motivate others and elevate them into their own unique direction.

In "Just A Thought," Byrd offers readers quotes and thoughts that would inspire them, ease their stress and motivate them to a positive direction. Moreover, he emphasizes how the book can help anyone to translate knowledge into reasonable and good decisions.

CPSIA information can be obtained
at www.ICGtesting.com
Printed in the USA
BVHW011201070323
659867BV00022B/789